Is it natural or human-made?

Helen Mason

Crabtree Publishing Company

www.crabtreebooks.com

Author: Helen Mason
Publishing plan research and development:
  Reagan Miller
Project development: Clarity Content Services
Project management: Joanne Chan
Project coordinator: Kathy Middleton
Editors: Rita Vanden Heuvel, Reagan Miller
Copy editor: Dimitra Chronopoulos
Proofreader: Kelly Spence, Kylie Korneluk
Design: Pixel Hive studio
Photo research: Linda Tanaka
Production coordinator and
    prepress technician: Tammy McGarr
Print coordinator: Margaret Amy Salter

Photographs:
Cover Shutterstock; p1 Julie Poulin/Thinkstock; p4 top Margo Harrison/Thinkstock, Ashka/ Shutterstock; p5 top Jovan Nikolic/Thinkstock, Pavel L Photo and Video/ Shutterstock; p6 Jupiter Images/Thinkstock; p7 top Getty Images/Thinkstock, Sari ONeal/Shutterstock; p8 top hudiemm/Thinkstock, Africanmoose/ Shutterstock; p9 Viktor Gladkov/Thinkstock; p10 top Sevaljevic/Thinkstock, Ramona Heim/Shutterstock; p11 Maksim Toome /Shutterstock, Fuse/ Thinkstock; p12 top Stockbyte/Thinkstock, Milosz M/Shutterstock; p13 top Gerald Bernard/Thinkstock, Bonita R. Cheshier/Shutterstock, TFoxFoto/Shutterstock; p14 top Blend Images/Thinkstock, saiva/Shutterstock, Lilia Barladyan/Shutterstock, Roblan/Shutterstock; p15 left Leslie Banks/Thinkstock, top right Julie Poulin/Thinkstock, sunstock/Thinkstock; p16 Iwona Grodzka/Thinkstock; p17 top Oleksandr Pekur/Thinkstock, Anton-Burakov/Shutterstock; p18 vikif/Thinkstock; p19 left Zelfit/Shutterstock, Pavel Ivanov/Thinkstock; p20 left Fexel/Shutterstock, Gary C. Tognoni/Shutterstock; p21 top clockwise Smileus/Thinkstock, Jennifer Barrow/Thinkstock, Viktoria Makarova/Thinkstock, Zoonar RF/Thinkstock; p22 left Andrey Kuzmin/Shutterstock, Paul Michael Hughes/Shutterstock.

Library and Archives Canada Cataloguing in Publication

Mason, Helen, 1950-, author
    Is it natural or human-made? / Helen Mason.

(What's the matter?)
Includes index.
Issued in print and electronic formats.
ISBN 978-0-7787-0535-2 (bound).--ISBN 978-0-7787-0539-0 (pbk.).--ISBN 978-1-4271-9024-6 (html).--ISBN 978-1-4271-9028-4 (pdf)

    1. Materials--Juvenile literature. 2. Synthetic products--Juvenile literature. 3. Raw materials--Juvenile literature. 4. Natural resources--Juvenile literature. 5. Matter--Properties--Juvenile literature. I. Title. II. Series: What's the matter? (St. Catharines, Ont.)

TA403.2.M383 2014   j620.1'1   C2014-900453-2
                                                             C2014-900454-0

Library of Congress Cataloging-in-Publication Data

Mason, Helen, 1950- author.
    Is it natural or human-made? / Helen Mason.
        pages cm. -- (What's the matter?)
    Includes index.
    ISBN 978-0-7787-0535-2 (reinforced library binding : alk. paper) -- ISBN 978-0-7787-0539-0 (pbk. : alk. paper) -- ISBN 978-1-4271-9024-6 (electronic html) -- ISBN 978-1-4271-9028-4 (electronic pdf)
    1. Materials--Appearance--Juvenile literature. 2. Natural products--Juvenile literature. 3. Synthetic products--Juvenile literature. 4. Matter--Properties--Juvenile literature. I. Title.

TA418.5.M37 2014
670--dc23
                                2014002266

Crabtree Publishing Company

www.crabtreebooks.com   1-800-387-7650

Printed in Canada/032014/MA20140124

Published in Canada
Crabtree Publishing
616 Welland Ave.
St. Catharines, ON
L2M 5V6

Published in the United States
Crabtree Publishing
PMB 59051
350 Fifth Avenue, 59th Floor
New York, New York 10118

Published in the United Kingdom
Crabtree Publishing
Maritime House
Basin Road North, Hove
BN41 1WR

Published in Australia
Crabtree Publishing
3 Charles Street
Coburg North
VIC 3058

What is in this book?

What is matter?

How are your
pet dog and
your backpack
the same?

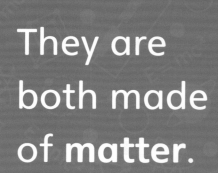

They are
both made
of **matter**.

All matter takes up space and has **mass**.

Mass is the amount of **material** in an object.

Everything around you is made of matter.

This includes the shoes on your feet and the people you meet.

What are properties?

Matter has **properties**.

Properties describe how something

looks, feels, tastes, smells, or sounds.

Your hair and clothes are different colors. Color is a property.

Trees are big and tall. Butterflies are small.

Size is a property too.

Is it natural or human-made?

Some things are found in nature.

These are **natural** materials.

Cotton is a plant. It is natural.

A bird is an animal. It is natural.

Some things are made by people. These are **human-made** materials.

Styrofoam is human-made.

The type of material something is made from is a property too.

Which words describe the properties of a tree leaf?

- big
- small
- green
- white
- natural
- human-made

Where do we find natural materials?

Some natural things grow.

Sheep grow a special hair called wool. Wool is natural.

People use the wool to make socks and hats.

These things are human-made.

Some natural things were always there. Rocks are natural.

Metal comes from rocks. It is found under the ground. We use metal to make cars.

What is made from natural materials?

Sometimes people change natural things. Trees are natural. People cut them down to get wood.

They use the wood to make useful **products**.

Products made from wood are human-made.

People make pumpkin pie.

The pumpkin is natural. The product is human-made.

People use rocks to build roads.

The rocks are natural. The product is human-made.

Human-made materials

Some things are made from human-made materials.

Plastic is human-made. It was first made in a **laboratory**.

A laboratory is a place where scientists test and make new things.

Many kinds of plastic are used to make toys, boots, and toothbrushes.

Nylon is human-made.

Umbrellas are made from nylon.

So are backpacks and cat toys.

Collect five plastic things. What properties does plastic have?

15

Natural and human-made

Some products are made from both natural and human-made materials.

The body of this puppet is wool.

The button eyes are plastic.

The body of this bicycle is metal.
The tires are rubber.

This umbrella is made from nylon.
The handle is wooden.

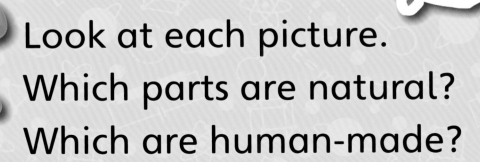

Look at each picture.
Which parts are natural?
Which are human-made?

Where is it made?

People bring natural materials to factories.

They change the materials to make products.

Wheat is a plant. Wheat seeds are ground into flour.

Flour is used to make bread.

Cotton plants are used to make cloth.
Cotton cloth is used to make clothes.

Oil is used to make plastic.
Toys are made from plastic.

List five things made in factories.

Is it natural or human-made?

How can you tell if something is natural or human-made? Use these clues.

Natural Things	Human-made Things
✓ grow ✓ are part of nature	✓ are made or built by humans ✓ start with natural objects that are changed

Which objects are natural? Which are human-made? What clues help you?

A

B

C

D

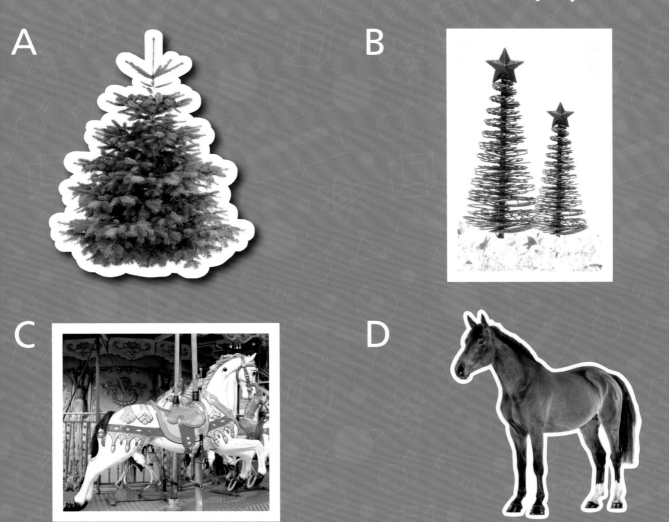

Natural you!

You are human. You are part of nature.

Humans grow. They are not made in factories.

We get many materials from nature. It is important to take care of nature.

Words to know and Index

human-made
pages 9, 10,
12–17, 20, 21

laboratory
page 14

mass
page 5

material
pages 5,
8, 9, 14,
16, 18

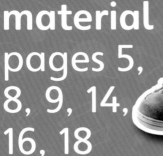

matter
pages 4–6

natural
pages 8-13,
16, 17, 18,
20, 21, 22

product
pages 12,
13, 16, 18

properties
pages 6–7,
9, 15

23

Notes for adults

Objectives
- to introduce the difference between natural and human-made objects
- to learn where human-made objects are made

Prerequisite
Ask the children to read *Is it heavy or light?* and *Is it hot or cold?* before reading *Is it natural or human-made?* These titles introduce the concept of matter and changes of state. They also discuss properties and how to use clues to classify objects.

Questions before reading *Is it natural or human-made?*
"What materials are part of nature?"

"What materials are made by humans?"

"Tell me about something you have helped grow."

"Is it natural or human–made?"

Discussion
Read the book with the children. Discuss with the children some of the main concepts in the book: natural and human-made, part of nature and made in a factory.

Show the children a real flower still growing in a pot and a plastic flower, also in a pot. Discuss the difference between the two objects. How might they care for the real flower? What about the plastic one?

Keep the two items over a period of time. Discuss the changes over time. What happens to the real flower? Does the same thing happen to the plastic one?

Extension
Have the children list a number of objects from their room or home. Challenge them to identify one object that is natural and one that is human-made. Discuss what clues they used to decide. How do they use the natural object? Can they determine what natural object(s) the human-made one was made from?